Summer Fun

Back to School

It was the first day of school.

Miss Gay was waiting at the door
of the Second Grade room.

"Hello," said Miss Gay. "I am glad
to see you. Did you have fun
this summer?"

"Yes," said the boys and girls.

"I want to hear about your summer fun,"
said Miss Gay.

6

"We went to a ranch," said Sam
and Kate.

"I went to a big city to see
my grandmother," said John.

"I went swimming with my father,"
said Henry. "We went on picnics, too."

"I went to see my uncle," said Tom.
"I watched men working on new houses
and new streets."

"Everyone had fun this summer,"
said Miss Gay. "You have been
many places. I have a map. Let's put
your names on the map to show where
you have been."

"May I put my name on an airplane?"
asked Sam. "That is the way we went
to the ranch."

"Yes," said Miss Gay. "We can show
how we traveled this summer, too."

"I would like to know more about what you did," said Miss Gay. "What can you bring to show us?"

"We can bring our cowboy hats," said Sam and Kate.

"I can bring something I bought in the city," said John.

"I have pictures of my fun at home," said Henry.

The children decided to bring things that would show where they had been.

10

Fun at a Ranch

The next day, Sam and Kate came
to school with cowboy hats and ropes.

They let the children play with them.

They told everyone
about their visit to the ranch.

Sam pointed to a spot on the map.
"This is where Kate and I went," he said.
"We went to a big town near the ranch."

"I know why you went in an airplane,"
said Billy. "You had a long way to go
and airplanes are very fast."

"Yes," said Kate. "It would
have taken two or three days in a car.
In the airplane, it took us
only six or seven hours."

"Uncle Jim and Aunt Nan met us
at the airport," said Sam. "It was
a long drive to their ranch. We drove
and drove without seeing any houses."

"Don't people live there?" asked Bob.

"Oh, yes," said Sam. "People live
there, but they live very far apart"

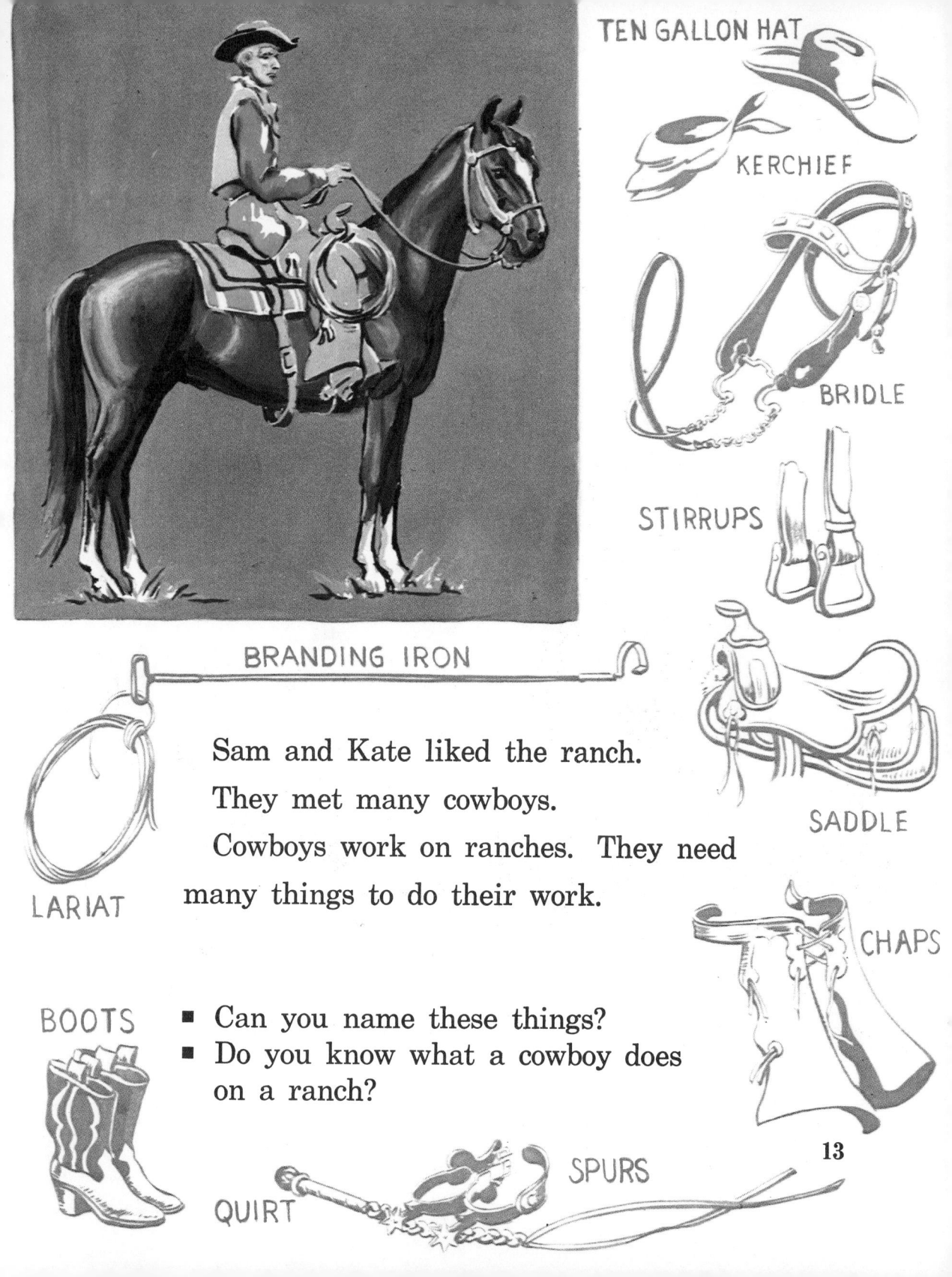

TEN GALLON HAT

KERCHIEF

BRIDLE

STIRRUPS

BRANDING IRON

SADDLE

LARIAT

Sam and Kate liked the ranch.

They met many cowboys.

Cowboys work on ranches. They need many things to do their work.

CHAPS

BOOTS

- Can you name these things?
- Do you know what a cowboy does on a ranch?

13

SPURS

QUIRT

Cowboys work very hard.

These pictures show some of the jobs

a cowboy must do.

- Can you think of any other jobs?
- Would you like to work on a ranch?
- What would you do in a day?

A Roundup

Uncle Jim asked Sam and Kate
if they would like to go on a roundup.

"I would like that," said Sam.

"All the neighbors are helping Mr. Long
with his roundup," said Uncle Jim. "They
will help me next week."

"What is a roundup?" asked Sam.

"Cowboys drive all the cattle
together in one place," said Uncle Jim.

"Then the ranchers count them. They
put a brand on each new calf."

"What is a brand?" asked Kate.

"Each rancher has a brand,"
said Uncle Jim. "It is a mark that
is put on all the cattle.

We can tell who owns the cattle
when they get lost. My brand is called
the Bar Z."

15

Early the next morning, Sam and Kate
left for the neighbor's ranch.

All day the men and horses worked
to round up the cattle.

They put a brand on each new calf.

Sometimes the calves would run away.
Sam helped to turn them back.

The cows and their calves
were put together.

Some of the cattle would be sold.

The other cattle were turned loose
to eat and grow larger.

17

Supplies for the Ranch

"One day I went to town
with Aunt Nan," said Kate.

"We were going to buy food and things
for the ranch. Aunt Nan doesn't go
to town every day. It is too far away.

The store had everything we needed.
We bought many things."

18

"We bought rope for Uncle Jim.
We bought a dress for Aunt Nan.
We bought boots for Sam and me.
   We bought all of the food
for the cowboys.
   There were many boxes and bags.
There was just enough room in the car
for Aunt Nan and me."

■ Why must Aunt Nan buy so much at once?
■ Is this store different from the one
   where your mother buys food?

Fun in the City

John told everyone
about his summer trip.

He had a surprise, too.

"I went to New York City," he said.
"Here it is on the map.

I went on a train. It took me
thirteen hours to get there.

I bought my supper on the train.
I slept on the train, too."

"Grandmother met me
at a big station," said John.

"We went to Grandmother's house
in a taxi. Grandmother lives
in a very tall house. In the city, people live
very close to each other."

"Where did you play?" asked Henry.

"We played in the street," said John.
"The policeman called our street
a play street. He did not let cars
use it.

On hot days, the policeman turned
on water for us. We liked that."

21

"I liked something else
in New York City," said John. "I liked
to ride on the subway."

"What is a subway?" asked Bob.

"A subway is a train that runs
under the ground. It goes very fast.

There are no cars and trucks to get
in the way. You can go many places
on the subway in New York City.

Hundreds and hundreds of people ride
the subway every day."

- Have you ever ridden on a subway?
- What do you think it would be like?

John showed the class his surprise.

It was a model of the Statue of Liberty.

"We went to see
the Statue of Liberty.

We went on a boat.

I climbed the steps to the top.

It was very high. I could see big boats
and big buildings all around."

A Neighborhood of New Houses

Tom brought some pictures to school.
They showed where he went this summer.

"I went to see my aunt and uncle,"
said Tom.

"Everything was new
in their neighborhood. There were
new houses as far as you could see.

They were building more new houses
and streets. I watched to see
how they did it."

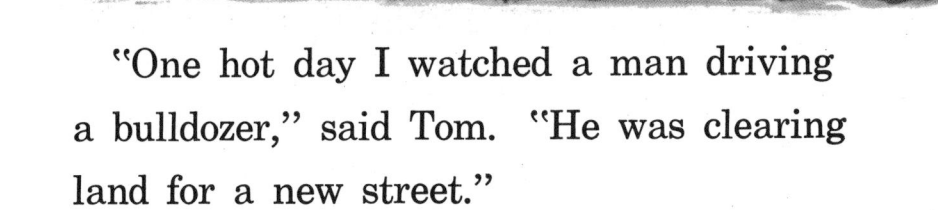

"One hot day I watched a man driving
a bulldozer," said Tom. "He was clearing
land for a new street."

"I would like to run a bulldozer,"
said Sam.

"That's just what I thought,"
said Tom. "But the man was working hard
and looked very hot.

That's when I had a wonderful
idea," said Tom. "I would take
some lemonade to the man!"

"Aunt Jane gave me a big glass
of lemonade," said Tom.

"I called to the man, but
he didn't hear me. I called again.

He stopped the bulldozer. I held
out the glass. He smiled and jumped
to the ground.

I gave him the lemonade. He liked
it. He said his name was Ben."

"Ben gave me a ride on the bulldozer.
I sat on the seat beside him.
When the bulldozer started,
it roared and jumped. I had a good time.
Ben and I were good friends.
I watched him many times. He told me
I must stay away from the bulldozer
when he wasn't there. It would not be
safe."

"You were lucky to have a ride
on a bulldozer," said Sam.

- Many men must work to build
  a new neighborhood.
- What are these men doing?
- Can you think of other jobs that must
  be done.

A Trailer Trip

"Miss Gay, we went away this summer.
We took our home with us," said Sally.

"You can't take your home on a trip,"
said Tom.

"We did," said Sally. "We bought
a house trailer and pulled it
with our car.

Our trailer is like a small house.
We have a living room. We have
two bedrooms. We have a bathroom.
There is a kitchen and a place to eat."

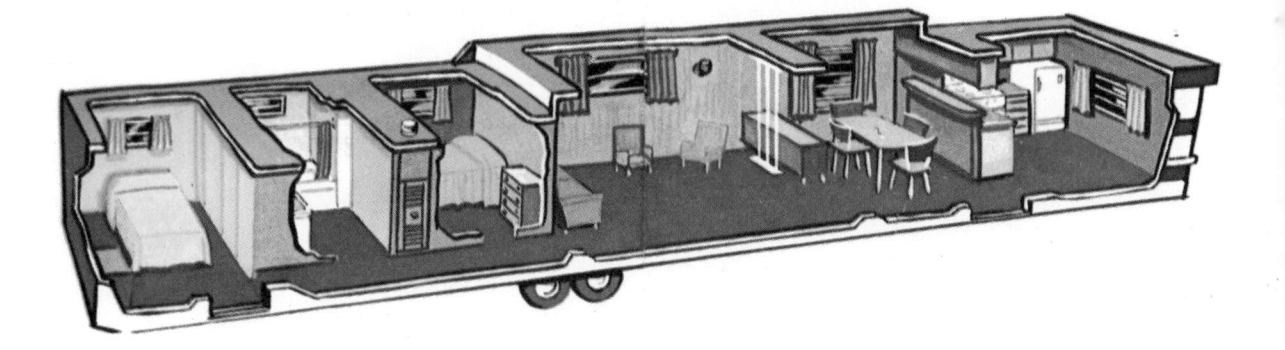

"Did you stay in a trailer park?"
asked Sam.

"Yes, and we went to many places,"
said Sally.

"We went to see the Grand Canyon.
It is one mile deep.

We saw the desert. It is very hot."

"One day we rode up a mountain,"
said Sally. "There were many big trees.
There was a fire tower on top
of the mountain. We climbed up
many steps to the top.

A forest ranger was there to watch
for forest fires. When he sees a fire,
he calls for help to put it out."

"I would like to be a forest ranger,"
said Henry. "It would be fun to help
put out fires."

"The ranger told us how everyone
could help," said Sally. "We must
be careful in the forest so we don't
start a forest fire."

■ Do you know how you must be careful
in a forest to prevent forest fires?

"Every day we took a trip," said Sally.
"At night we always came back
to the trailer to sleep.
We had a good vacation."

■ Would you like this kind
of a vacation? Why?

Fun at Home

"Miss Gay, I had fun at home this summer," said Henry. "I have some pictures of what I did.

We went swimming. We cooked in our backyard.

I had fun in the library.

Daddy took me to see a rocket. A soldier told us about the rocket."

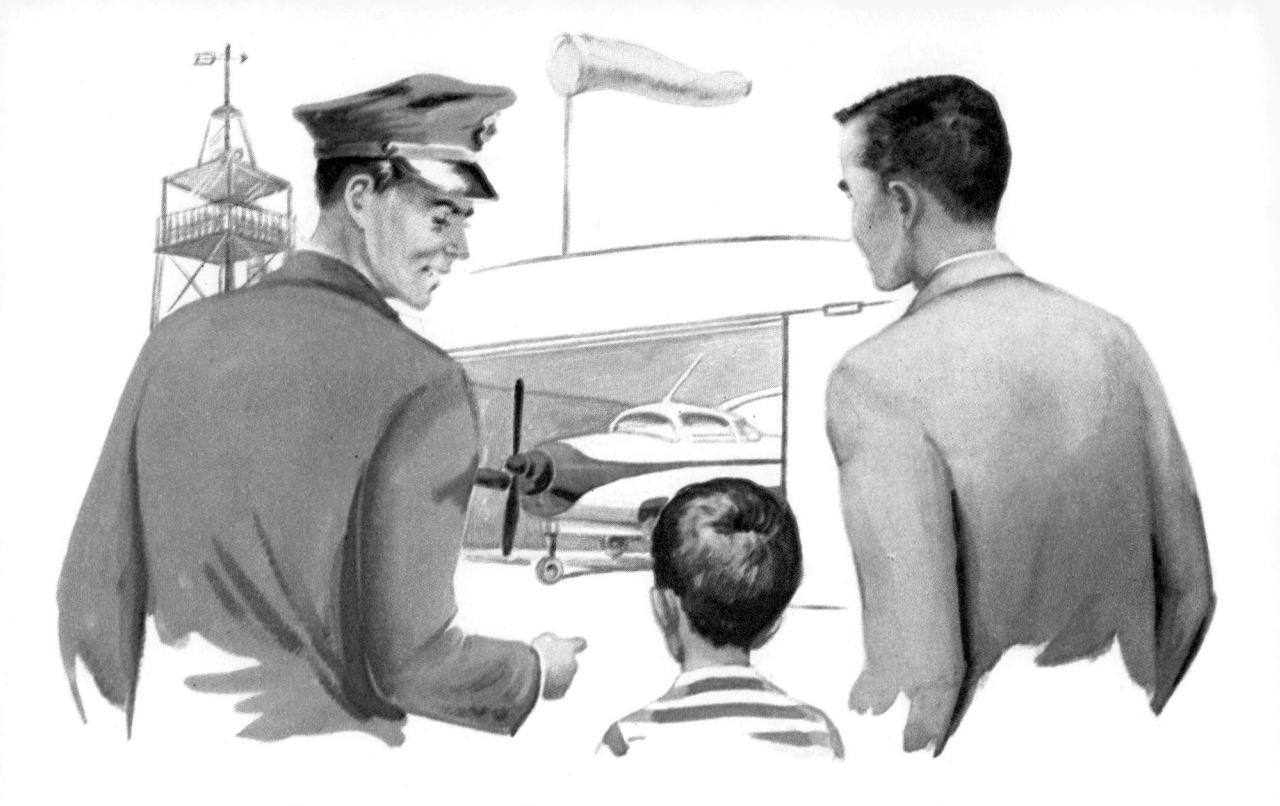

"On my birthday, we went to the airport," said Henry. "We saw many things.

We saw the airplane hangars.

We visited the control tower. Men tell the planes when to land and take off. Their job is very important.

Then came a surprise. Mr. Sands, a pilot, took us over to a beautiful blue and white airplane.

We climbed in and waited for the control tower to tell us when to take off."

"Up and up we went. It was fun.

I could look down and see my house.

I saw the school, too. I saw

the whole town."

"That was a wonderful birthday

surprise," said Miss Gay.

"You all had a wonderful summer."

- What did you do this summer?
- If you went away, how did you travel?
- What did you do to have fun at home
  this summer?

Neighbors

During the summer, the children
in the Second Grade visited many different
kinds of neighborhoods.

Sam and Kate visited a ranch
where neighbors live far apart.

John visited a big city where
neighbors live close together.

Tom visited a new neighborhood.
Everything was new. There were
new houses, new streets, and new neighbors.

Sally's neighborhood was a trailer
park. Her family had many different
neighbors, who lived in trailers, too.

Miss Gay and the Second Grade children
live in Greenwood.

Greenwood is a town where people
live together as neighbors.

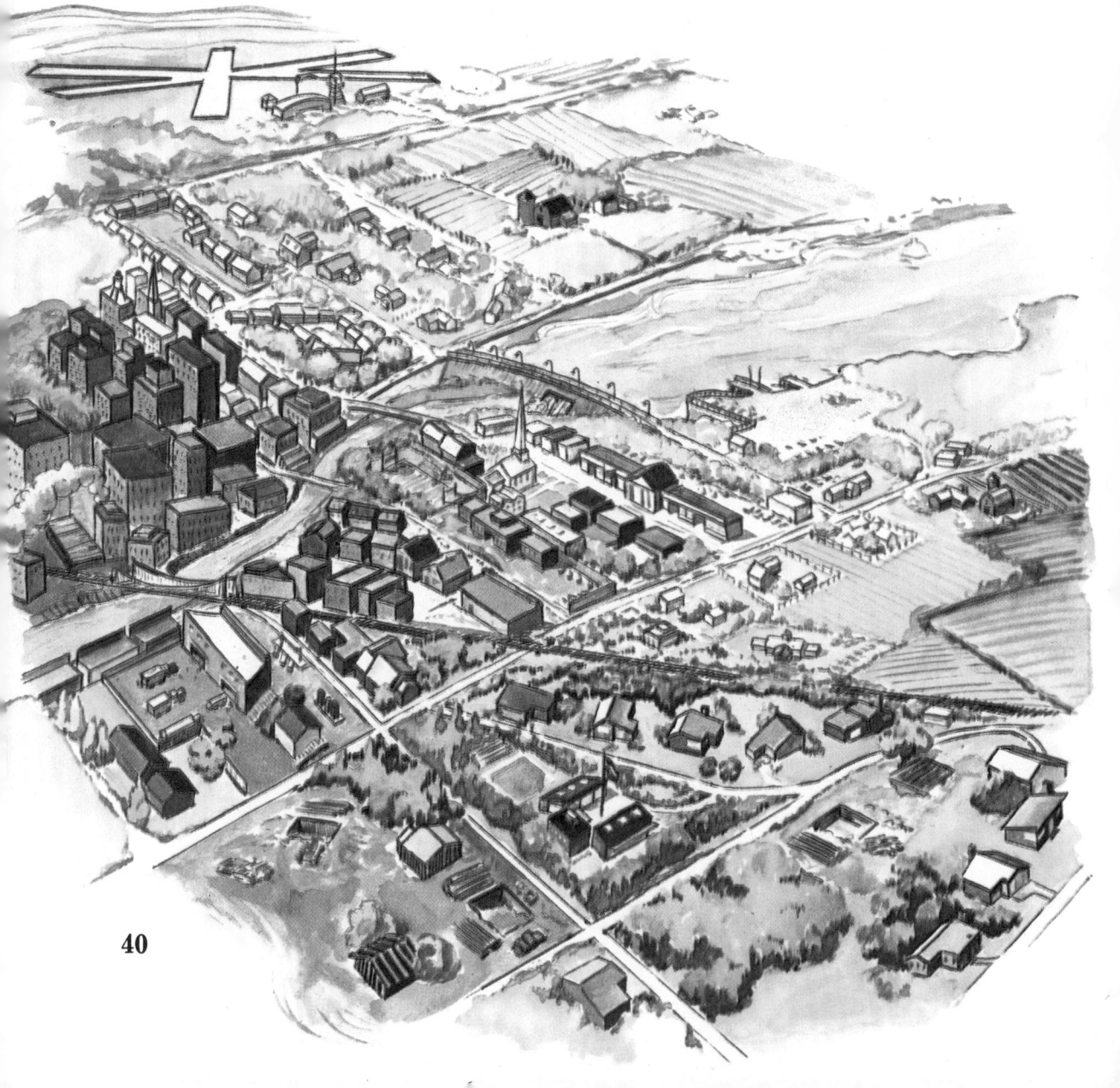

In Greenwood, there are different kinds of neighborhoods.

Some people live close together in apartment houses.

Some people live in one family houses. Sometimes there are yards between the houses.

Sometimes the houses are built close together.

In Greenwood there are
new neighbors too.

Near Greenwood people
live on farms. They do not
live close together. They
need room for their farms.

- Are any of these neighborhoods
  like yours?
- How are these neighborhoods alike?

42

The people who live in Greenwood help each other. This is what neighbors are for.

When people live together they need many things.

Neighbors do different things to help each other.

- How are these people helping each other?
- Can you think of other ways people help each other?
- Are you a good neighbor?
- How do you help your neighbors?

Miss Gay and the Second Grade
talked about the things people
in Greenwood need.

They talked about the neighbors
who helped them get what they need.

- Can you think of some things people
  in your city or town need?
- What neighbors help people get
  these things?

Food for Greenwood

Everyone needs food.

Many people help us get the food
we need.

In this part of the book, the Second Grade
will learn about the people
who help them get food.

They will meet neighbors who live
in Greenwood.

They will learn about other people
who live far away.

- As you read these stories,
  think about these things:
- Think about the many kinds of food
  you like.
- Think about the neighbors in your
  city or town who help you get food.
- Think about the places these foods
  come from.
- Think about the people who help
  get these foods to you.

A Visit to a Supermarket

One morning Sue had some good news
for the Second Grade.

"I talked to my father last night,"
she said. "He said that many people work
to help us get our food.

He works in a supermarket. He said
we could come to visit the supermarket."

"That would be fun," said Miss Gay.

"I go to the supermarket
with my mother," said Sam.

"I do too," said many of the children.

"But you don't go into the storerooms,"
said Sue.

"What will we see in the storerooms?"
asked Tom.

"Many things," said Sue. "You will
find out when we go."

"I will ask the principal if we may go
to the supermarket," said Miss Gay.

"Then I will talk to Sue's father
about our visit."

- Do you go with your family
  to the supermarket?
- What do you like best
  about the supermarket?
- Have you been to the storerooms
  in the supermarket?
- What do you think the Second Grade
  will see?

The Supermarket

Mr. Johnson, Sue's father, met
the Second Grade at the door.

"Good morning," he said. "Miss Gay
told me you want to see how we work
in the supermarket. Most of the work
is done in the storerooms."

The Second Grade followed Mr. Johnson.
He opened the doors at the back
of the store.

"Let's go downstairs," he said.
"There is something I want to show you."

49

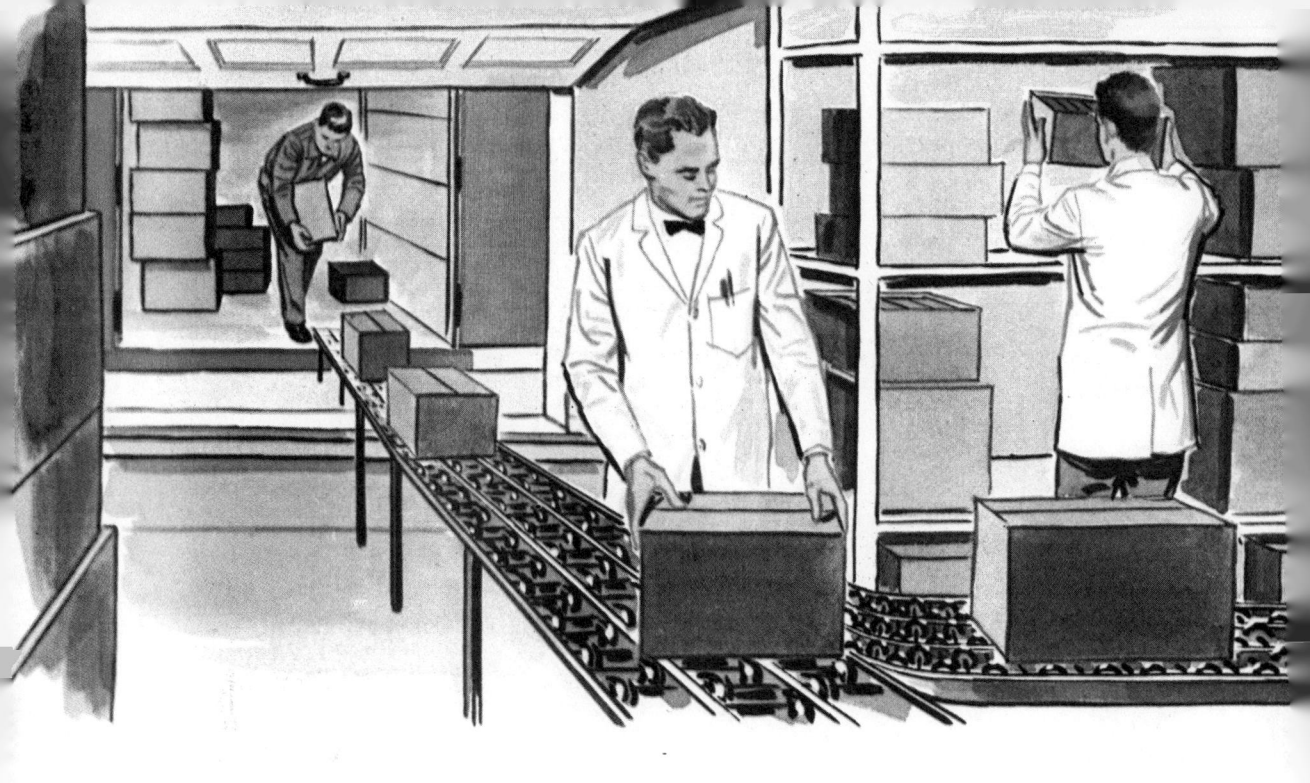

Down the stairs went Mr. Johnson
and the Second Grade.

The big storeroom under the supermarket
was filled with boxes.

A big truck had just come. Men
were helping to unload.

Swish, swish came the many boxes
down the long slide.

Around the room went the boxes.

Some men opened the boxes. Other men
put the prices on the groceries.

"Come with me," said Mr. Johnson. "Let's see how the men get the groceries upstairs to the main floor. Bill is going to send some boxes up now."

Bill put four boxes on a moving belt.

"That machine saves us a lot of work," said Mr. Johnson.

Mr. Johnson opened the door
to a large room.

"In this room, are the machines
that keep our refrigerators cold," he said.

"You must have many refrigerators,"
said Sam.

"We do," laughed Mr. Johnson. "There are
twenty machines in this room. We need
them all to keep our refrigerators cold."

- Why does the supermarket need
  so many refrigerators?
- What foods do they keep
  in the refrigerators?
- Do you think the refrigerators
  in the supermarket are like the one
  in your home?

The Refrigerators

Mr. Johnson showed the children
a large refrigerator. "We keep ice cream
and frozen food here," he said.

"Can I walk into this refrigerator?"
asked Sam.

"Yes," said Mr. Johnson. "Go right in."

Sam took two steps in. He turned and
ran out. "Whew! That is cold," he said.

"It is very cold," laughed Mr. Johnson.

EMERGENCY
ALARM

"The men don't stay long
in this refrigerator. They are careful
not to let the door close
when they are inside," said Mr. Johnson.

"What do they do if the door closes?"
asked Tom.

"There is a bell they can ring,"
said Mr. Johnson. "Someone will hear
the bell and open the door.

If no one hears the bell, they can use
the ax to cut through the door."

Mr. Johnson opened another door.
"This refrigerator is for fresh fruits
and vegetables," he said. "We keep
the fresh foods here until we need
them upstairs. This refrigerator
does not get very cold."

"Where do you keep the meat?" asked Tom.

"I will take you to the meat room now,"
said Mr. Johnson.

In the meat room, men were busy
cutting the meat.

"This refrigerator is just cold enough
to keep the meat fresh,"
said Mr. Johnson.

55

"The meat comes to us in big pieces," said Mr. Johnson.

"These men cut the meat so people can buy what they want.

These men are called butchers."

- Do you know where this meat comes from?
- Do you know how it gets to the supermarket?
- What tools do the butchers use in their work?

Produce for the Supermarket

Before the children left, a truck
came to the supermarket.

"The produce truck is here,"
called a man.

"Produce is what we call
fruits and vegetables," said Mr. Johnson.
"We can watch the men unload
the produce."

"Look at the oranges," said Sue.

"They have come a long way
to Greenwood," said Miss Gay.

"The oranges came from California
and Florida," said Miss Gay.

"That is where most of our oranges
are grown," said Mr. Johnson.
"Oranges will not grow where it is cold.

When it does get cold, the farmers
must keep the orange trees warm.
They build fires to keep the trees warm."

■ Can you tell how oranges get
  to the supermarket?
■ Do you know other kinds of fruits
  that come from warm places?

"Look at what those men are doing,"
called Kate.

"We wash our fresh vegetables,"
said Mr. Johnson.

"We must cut the bad leaves
from the lettuce.

We must make sure all the produce
is clean and fresh."

Before the Second Grade left,
Mr. Johnson gave them a box wrapped
in white paper. On the box it said—

For the Second Grade
Do not open until after lunch

"Thank you," said Miss Gay
and the children.

The Surprise

After lunch, Miss Gay opened the box.
She held it so everyone could see.

"Oh, boy," shouted Sam.
"Chocolate candy!"

"What a nice surprise," said Miss Gay.
"Everyone can have a piece."

"I wonder where the candy
came from," said Mary.

"Last summer I went to a place
where chocolate candy is made,"
said Miss Gay.

"Tell us about it," said Mary.

"The story of chocolate starts
with a tree," said Miss Gay. "This tree
is called the cacao tree.

Cacao trees are different from any
you have ever seen. They grow
in countries far away
where it is hot all the time.

Big pods grow on these trees.
Inside the pods are the cacao beans.
Chocolate is made from these beans."

"Did they make this candy there, too?"
asked Mary.

"No," said Miss Gay. "Many people
in many different places worked hard
so you could enjoy this candy."

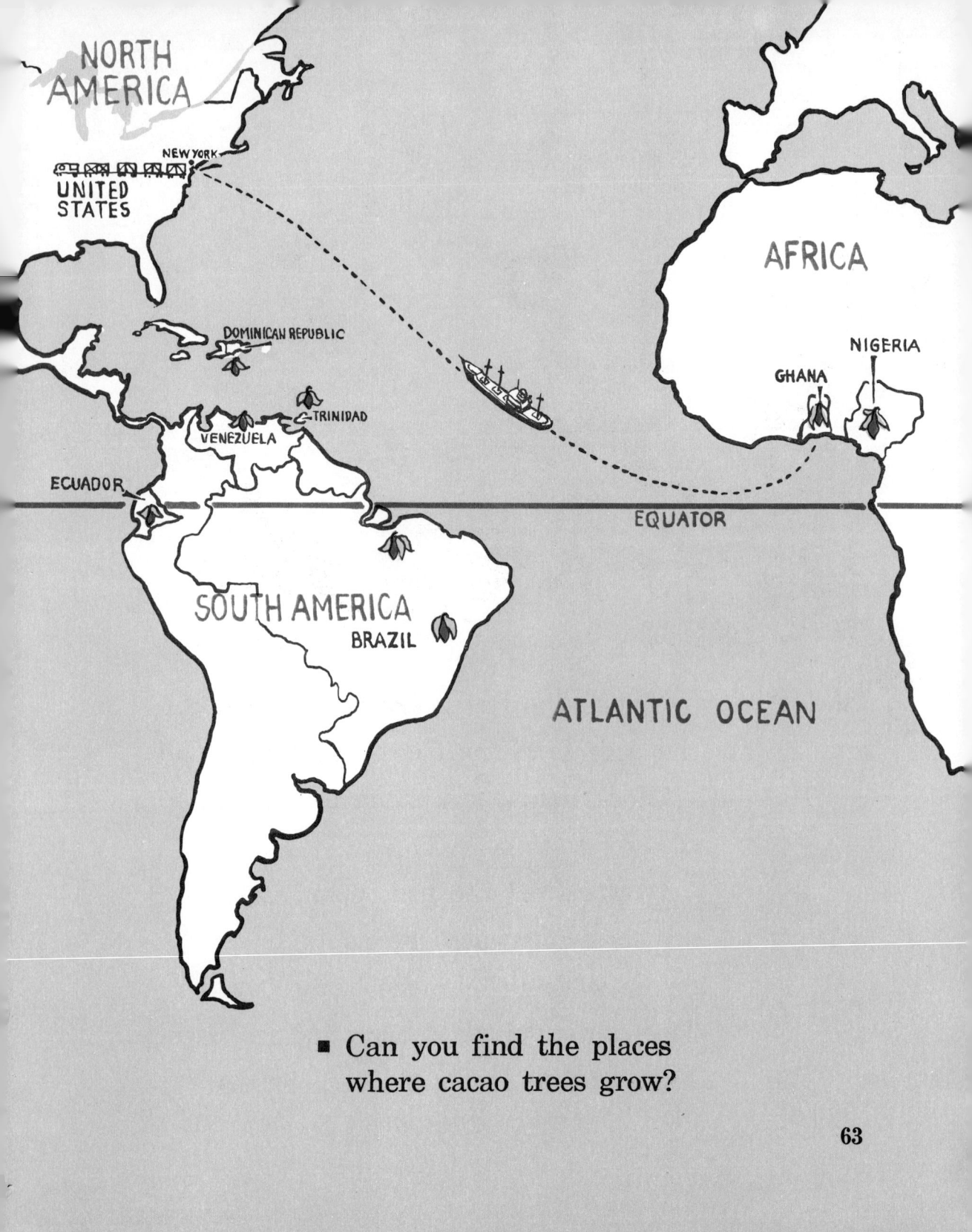

NORTH AMERICA

UNITED STATES

NEW YORK

DOMINICAN REPUBLIC

TRINIDAD

VENEZUELA

ECUADOR

EQUATOR

SOUTH AMERICA

BRAZIL

AFRICA

NIGERIA

GHANA

ATLANTIC OCEAN

■ Can you find the places
where cacao trees grow?

"When the beans are ready, men cut
the pods from the trees," said Miss Gay.

"Each man has a knife on the end
of a long stick.

Workers cut the pods open. Inside
are the white cacao beans.

The workers take the beans out.
They put them on the ground in the sun.
As they dry, the beans turn brown."

"It takes many days for the beans
to dry. Each day someone must turn the
beans. The workers walk through the
beans and turn them with their feet.

When the cacao beans are dry, they
are put in big bags. Then they are ready
for a long trip across the ocean.

Ships take the beans to places
where they will be made into candy
and other good things to eat."

"When the ships get to this country,"
said Miss Gay, "the beans are put
on trains. The trains take the beans
to the candy factory.

At the candy factory, the beans
are cleaned and put into very hot ovens.

Machines break the beans into smaller
and smaller pieces.

Heat melts the small pieces of beans.

Then a dark brown liquid runs out
of the machines. This is called
cocoa butter. It smells very good."

"Can you eat cocoa butter?" asked Sam.

"It is not sweet," said Miss Gay.
"Two things must be put
into the cocoa butter to make candy."

"Sugar makes it sweet," said Kate.
"They put sugar in the cocoa butter."

"Yes," said Miss Gay. "They must put
sugar and milk into the cocoa butter.

First the milk and sugar
are cooked together.

Then they are put
into the cocoa butter. Big machines
mix and mix the chocolate.

Then it is made into candy bars
like those we ate today."

- Can you tell who these people are?
- Can you think of others who help?
- Cocoa beans come from far away. Name some other foods that come from far away.

Bread for Greenwood

Sam came into the kitchen.

"Look at the rain," he said.

Mother was getting breakfast.
There was orange juice, eggs,
bread with butter and jam, and milk.

"Did you buy all these things
at the supermarket?" asked Sam.

"No," said Mother.

"A man brings our milk to the house,"
said Kate.

"Mr. Taylor brings our bread
to the house," said Father.

"Yes," said Mother. "I get our food
from many different places."

69

- Do you have stores like these in your city or town?
- Where else can you buy food in your city or town?

The doorbell rang. It was Mr. Taylor.
He had just brought some fresh bread.

"Good morning, Mr. Taylor," said Sam
and Kate.

"Would you like to ride in my truck?"
asked Mr. Taylor. "It is raining hard.
I am going by the school."

"Oh, yes," said Sam. "Could we ride
in Mr. Taylor's truck, Mother?"

"Yes," said Mother. "You will not
have to walk to school in the rain."

"Let's go," said Mr. Taylor.

Mr. Taylor's truck was filled with good
things to eat. There was fresh bread.
There were cakes and pies and cookies.

"It smells good in here," said Kate.

"Where did you get all of these cakes
and things?" asked Sam.

"I got them at the bakery downtown,"
said Mr. Taylor. "That is where they
were made."

"A bakery is a factory where bread
and cakes are made," said Sam.

"Well, it is a kind of factory,"
laughed Mr. Taylor. "We call it
a bakery because we bake the things
we make."

GREENWOOD BAKERY

"The people who work there are
called bakers.

We have many bakers at our bakery,"
said Mr. Taylor.

"People in Greenwood want bread
and cakes. The bakers work all night
to make enough for everyone."

"Why do they work at night?"
asked Kate.

"They want the bread to be fresh
for the people each morning,"
said Mr. Taylor.

"If we wanted to see the bakers,
we would have to stay up all night,"
said Sam.

"Yes," laughed Mr. Taylor,
"they work while you are asleep."

Soon they were at school. "Here is
a little book that tells
all about bread," said Mr. Taylor.

"It will tell you how the bakers
make bread."

"Thank you," said Sam and Kate.

Sam and Kate hurried into the school
to show the book to Miss Gay.

"Take off your coats and boots,"
she said. "Then we can look
at your book."

■ Now you can read the book
with Miss Gay and the Second Grade.

The Story of Bread

The farmer plants the wheat
with big machines.

During the warm summer, the wheat
grows. It turns a light brown.
Then the farmer knows it is ready
to cut.

The farmer uses a big machine
to cut the wheat. The machine
also knocks the seeds from each plant.

75

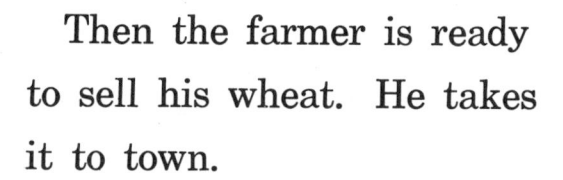

Then the farmer is ready
to sell his wheat. He takes
it to town.

A train takes the wheat
to big flour mills. At the flour mills,
big machines clean and wash the wheat.
Then it is ground into flour.

The flour goes from the mill
to many cities and towns. It goes
by truck and trains. Some of it
goes to stores. Some of it goes
to bakeries.

At the bakeries, the flour
is made into bread and other
good things to eat. Everything
is kept very clean. First,
the flour is made into dough.

Big machines turn and mix the dough.
Around and around they turn.

Then the dough is put in a warm room.
The yeast in the dough makes it rise.
The dough becomes bigger and bigger.
Soon it fills the pan.

A machine cuts the dough into loaves.
A man puts the loaves into pans.

The loaves are put in the big oven.

When the bread is cooked, the loaves
come out of the oven. Next the loaves
are cut and wrapped to keep them fresh.
Then off they go to homes and to stores.

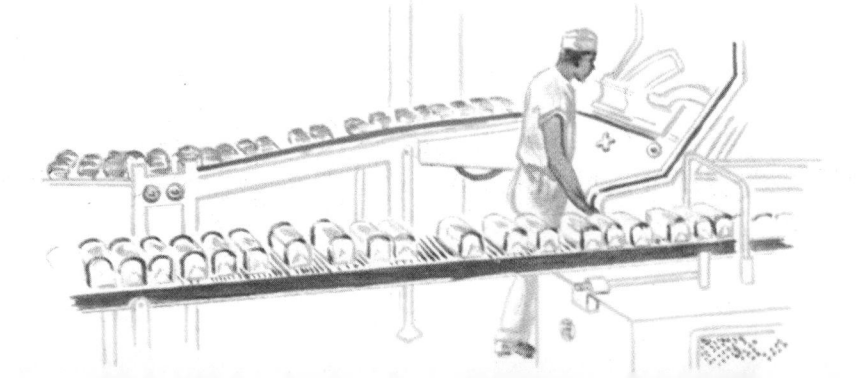

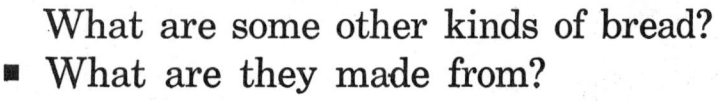

- Can you name all of the people
  who help you get bread?
- Why does it take so many people?
- We have read about wheat bread.
  What are some other kinds of bread?
- What are they made from?

Bread Long Ago

"That was a good story," said Miss Gay.

"I didn't know they had a machine to mix the dough," said Sue. "At home my mother mixes the dough with her hands."

"She doesn't mix as much as they do at the bakery," said Miss Gay.

"It would be very hard to mix that much dough by hand.

We have not always had machines for making bread. People didn't buy as much bread long ago. They made their bread at home."

"Sometimes my mother makes bread at home," said Sue.

"Long ago, mothers made bread every week," said Miss Gay. "There were no bakeries where they could buy bread.

Baking day was fun. Everyone helped.

Early in the morning, a big pile of wood was put by the stove. A fire had to be kept going all day long.

The dough was mixed and put in pans.

When the loaves had risen, they were put in the oven. The good smell made everyone hungry."

"When the loaves were a beautiful
brown, they were taken out of the oven.
After they had cooled, everyone
had a piece of bread with butter and jam."

"That story makes me hungry," said Sam.

"Maybe we could make bread sometime,"
said Miss Gay.

"Do you know how to make bread?"
asked Kate.

"Yes," said Miss Gay. "My grandmother
showed me how she made bread long ago."

This is how the Second Grade made bread.

THINGS THEY USED

1 🥣 and ¼ 🥣 of warm water
  cups

1 ✉ dry yeast
  package

2 🥄 🥄 soft shortening
  teaspoons

2 🥄 🥄 salt
  teaspoons

2 🥄 🥄 sugar
  tablespoons

3 🥣 🥣 🥣 flour
  cups

sift flour before putting into cups

83

Mix yeast in water.

Add shortening, salt, sugar, and half
of the flour.

Mix 300 times with a ⌒⌒⌒⌒⌒⌒◯ .

Keep dough off the sides of the bowl.

Add other half of the flour.

Mix with a ⌒⌒⌒⌒⌒⌒◯ .

Cover with a cloth.

Put dough in a warm place
for 30 minutes. Look for a surprise.

Beat dough 25 times.

Put in greased loaf pan.

Put pan in a warm place for 40 minutes.
There will be another surprise.

Put in oven (375°).

Bake for 45 to 50 minutes until brown.

Remove from pans. Let cool.

- What was the surprise?
- Do you know what caused the surprise?
- Why do we put yeast in bread?

Clothes
for Greenwood

It takes many people to help us
get the clothes we need.

In this part of the book the Second Grade
will learn about some of these people
in Greenwood.

They will learn how thread is made
from many different things.

They will learn how shirts are made
in a factory.

They will learn how clothes
were made a long time ago.

- As you read these stories,
  think about these things:
- Think about the different kinds
  of clothes you need.
- Think about the people in your city
  or town who help you get
  these clothes.
- Think about the different kinds
  of stores that sell clothes.
- Think about the places where the stores
  get the clothes they sell.

New Clothes for Henry

It was Saturday. Henry and his mother
stood on a busy corner in Greenwood.

They were waiting to cross the street.

They were going to Mr. Newman's store.

The traffic light changed
and they crossed the street safely.

Mr. Newman's store had clothes
for men and boys. It was a busy place
on Saturday morning.

"Good morning," called Mr. Newman.
"I will help you soon."

87

Henry and his mother looked
at many things. Henry found the coats.

"May I try them on?" he asked.

"Yes, you may," said Mr. Newman.
"Do you see one you like?"

"I like that brown one," said Henry.

"I think it will be a good fit,"
said Mr. Newman. "Let's try it on."

It was a good fit. Henry and
his mother liked it.

"How much does it cost?" asked Henry.

"This coat is twenty dollars,"
said Mr. Newman.

"That's a lot of money," said Henry.

"Yes," said Mr. Newman. "This is a good wool coat. It takes a lot of money to make a coat like this.

Many people worked on this coat. They must be paid for their work."

"Oh," said Henry. "The money we pay for this coat will pay everyone who worked on it."

"Yes," laughed Mr. Newman. "You must pay everyone who helps you get a fine coat like this."

Henry and his mother told Mr. Newman they would take the coat.

"Henry needs some shirts, too,"
said Henry's mother.

"We have some shirts you will like,"
said Mr. Newman. "They were made
at the new shirt factory in Greenwood."

Henry and his mother bought two shirts.

Mr. Newman put the new clothes
in a box. "Thank you," he said.
"I hope you will like wearing
your new coat and shirts."

"I know I will," said Henry.

"Good-by."

These people helped with Henry's coat.

The men who took care
of the sheep were given
money for the wool.

People who made
the wool cloth were paid
for their work.

People who made the coat
from the cloth were paid
for their work.

Men who drove
these trucks were paid
for their work.

People who sell
the coats are paid
for their work.

■ Can you think of all the people
who helped with your shoes?

Clothes Are Made from Many Things

Henry showed Miss Gay his new shirt.
"It is made of nylon and cotton," he said.
"It doesn't have to be ironed
because it has nylon in it."

"Did your mother make your shirt?"
asked Miss Gay.

"No, we bought it downtown
at Mr. Newman's store," said Henry.
"He said it was made in Greenwood
at the new shirt factory."

"I would like to see how they make
shirts," said Miss Gay. "We can visit
the factory. Would you like that?"

"I would," said Henry.

"I have a new coat, too," said Henry.
"It is made of wool. Wool comes
from sheep."

"I have a silk dress," said Kate.
"How do we get silk?"

"A silkworm makes the thread,"
said Miss Gay. "Men take the silk thread
and make cloth."

"Henry's shirt is made of nylon and cotton.

I want to know about nylon and cotton,"
said Sue.

"I can tell you about cotton,"
said Bob.

"My grandfather is a farmer. He has
a cotton farm. He has big fields
of cotton on his farm."

"Cotton is a plant that grows
where there are long warm summers,"
said Miss Gay.

"Yes," said Bob. "It was very hot
when I visited my grandfather last summer.

He showed me the cotton plants. I saw
green buds growing on the plants.
These are called cotton bolls.

The bolls grew bigger and bigger
during the summer.

When the bolls burst open, the fields
looked like they were covered with snow.

Then the cotton is ready to be picked."

Men pick the cotton.

It is fun to ride
to town on the cotton.

The cotton goes to a place
where machines take the seeds
out of the cotton.

The cotton goes
to a mill to be made
into thread and cloth.

"Where does nylon come from?"
asked Sue.

"Nylon does not come from plants
and animals," said Miss Gay. "It is
made by men. It is called man-made.

Nylon is made from such things
as coal, oil, air, and water.

Men put these things together
and heat them. Something brand new
is made.

This is pushed through small holes.
As it comes through the holes, it dries
and makes strong nylon thread.

These threads are used to make cloth
just like all other threads.

Sometimes nylon thread is mixed
with another kind of thread. Henry's
shirt is made of nylon thread
and cotton thread. My sweater is made
of nylon thread and wool thread."

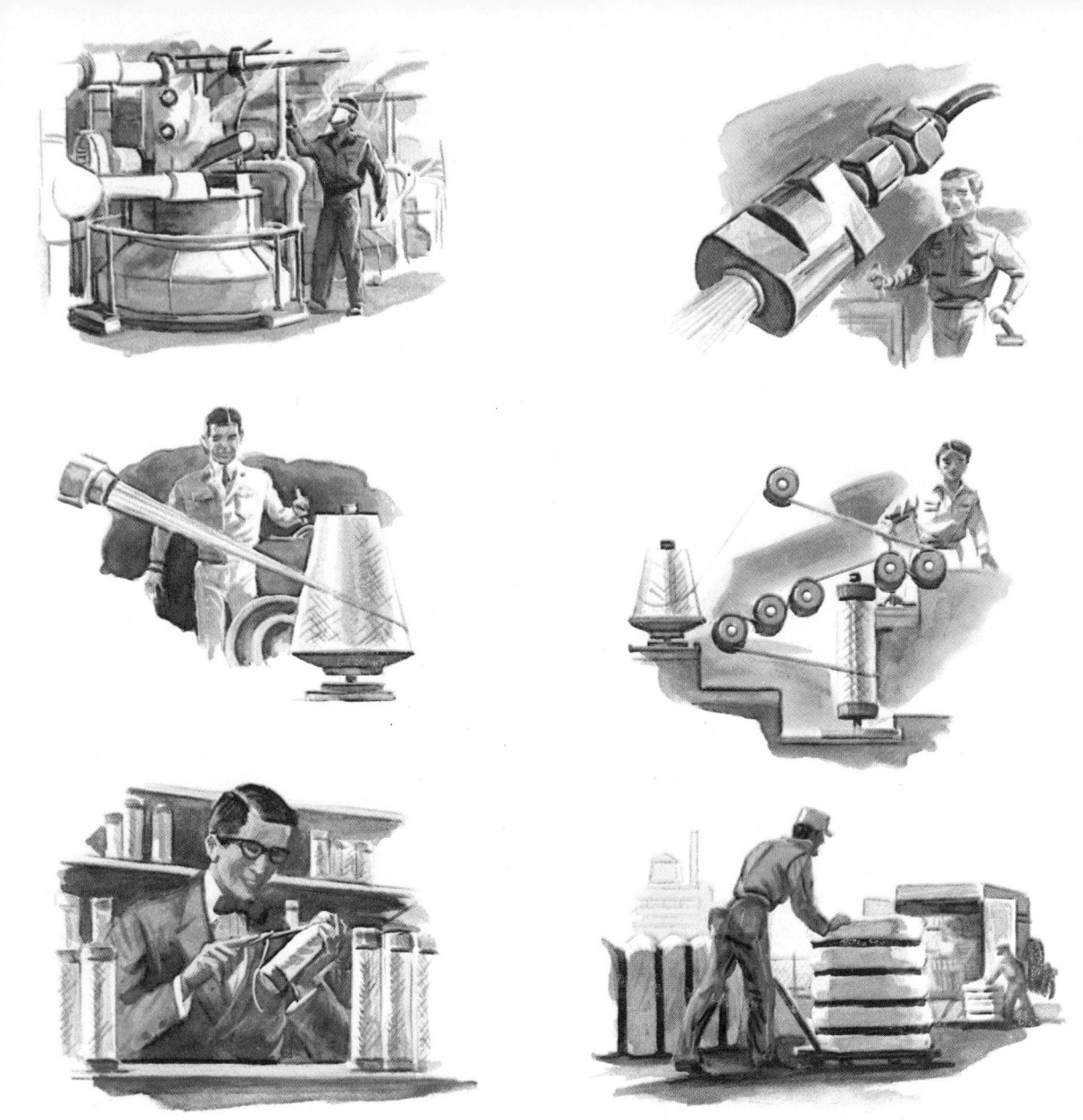

- What kind of cloth are your clothes made from?
- How many different kinds of cloth are there in your classroom today?

A Visit to the Shirt Factory

Miss Gay and the children planned their trip to the shirt factory. They thought of things they wanted to know.

They asked Sally's mother to go with them.

At last the day came. They all got on the bus and away they went.

At the factory, they were met by the foreman. He was going to show them the factory.

They went into a big noisy room.

Henry said, "Look at that big pile of cloth on the table. What is the man going to do with that?"

"He will cut that into shirts," said the foreman.

"I'll bet he has big scissors," said Sam.

"Watch him," said the foreman. "He doesn't use scissors. He uses an electric cutter."

"How does he know where to cut?" asked Kate.

"He puts chalk marks on the cloth," said the foreman.

"He must be very careful," said Miss Gay. "One wrong cut and a lot of cloth would be spoiled."

"Here are the people who sew
the shirts," said the foreman.

"How big the sewing machines are,"
said Sue.

"We must have big ones,"
said the foreman.

"Each worker sews a different part
of the shirt."

"Why doesn't one worker sew
the whole shirt?" asked Henry.

"This way is faster," said the foreman.
"That machine sews on the buttons."

"There are machines for everything,"
said John.

The foreman took them to another room.
People were putting the shirts into boxes.

"We can see that it takes many people
to make a shirt," said Miss Gay.

"I didn't know they made so many shirts
at one time," said Henry.

"By making many shirts at one time,
they can sell the shirts for less money,"
said Miss Gay.

"Without machines, it would take
one person a long time to make a shirt.
Then we would have to pay more money
for it."

"Thank you for showing us the way
you make shirts," said Miss Gay.

"Yes, thank you," said the Second Grade.

On the way back to school, Miss Gay
told the Second Grade about making
clothes long ago.

"A long time ago people did not have
machines. They had to make their clothes
by hand. They had to make the cloth
for their shirts and dresses."

- Have you ever seen anyone make a shirt
  or dress?
- Tell how they made it.
- How is this different from the way
  Henry's shirt was made?

Clothes Long Ago

Hope and Will had come to live
in the big woods three years ago.
There were no families near them.

Father had cut down trees and made
a warm log house.

Mother had taught Hope and Will how
to read and write.

Soon other families moved
into the big woods. Then they had
neighbors. Soon there were enough children
to build a school.

103

All the neighbors worked together.
The men and boys cut the logs to build
the school. The women and girls cooked
food for them to eat while they worked.

With everyone working together,
it did not take long to build
the new log schoolhouse.

When the new teacher arrived, everyone
would be at the school to meet him.

There was going to be a picnic.
It would be fun.

Hope and Will were busy getting ready for school.

Will was making a fur hat.

Hope was working to finish the cloth for her new dress.

Last spring Father and Will had cut the wool from the sheep.

Mother and Hope had washed and cleaned the wool.

Then they combed the wool to make it straight. This is called carding.

105

A spinning wheel was used to make
the thread. Hope could spin
good strong thread. She knew just how
to twist the wool as the wheel turned.

When she had enough thread, she began
to make the cloth for her dress.
She sat at the loom and wove
the threads back and forth.
It took a long time to weave enough
cloth for a dress.

One day Hope said to her mother,
"I think I will finish the cloth today.
Can we dye it tomorrow?"

"Yes," said her mother. "Do you have
the nuts we will need to make the dye?"

"Will and I picked a bag full,"
said Hope.

The next afternoon, Hope and her mother
made the dye from the nuts.

They put the cloth in the hot dye.

When the cloth was a beautiful yellow,
they took it out to dry.

Then her mother began to make
the new dress.

All this time, Will had been working on his fur hat.

He caught a raccoon in a trap in the woods. His father showed him how to remove the skin and dry it.

The skin was very hard when it was dry. To make the skin soft, Will rubbed and worked it with his hands. He did this for a very long time.

When it was very soft, his father helped him make a beautiful hat.

- What machines did Hope use in making the cloth?
- Why did it take Will a long time to make his hat?
- Can you find another story about making cloth long ago?

A New Hat and a New Dress

The new dress and hat were ready
in time for the picnic. How fine
everyone looked.

Everyone was happy as they set out
for the new schoolhouse.

Mother had cooked many good things
to take to the picnic. She carried
them in a big basket.

It was not a long walk. This would be
the way Hope and Will would go
to school.

At the schoolhouse, Hope and Will
found the other children.
What fun they had playing with everyone.

Everyone tried to guess
how the new schoolteacher would look.
Would he be tall? Would he be short?
Would he be —

Just then, the new schoolteacher
walked through the trees. He was tall.
He was smiling.

"Hello," everyone called.

Will knew he would like
the new teacher. He was wearing a hat
just like the one Will had made.

- Would you like to have lived long ago
  with Hope and Will? Why?
- Can you tell a story
  about this long ago time?

People Who Work
for Greenwood

Many people help us have
a better place in which to live.

They work to put out fires.

They work to keep us safe.

They work to keep our streets
and parks clean.

In this part of the book,
the Second Grade will learn
about these people in Greenwood.

These people work for Greenwood.

They will learn how these people
are paid by Greenwood.

- As you read these stories,
  think about these things:
- Think about the people in your city
  or town who work to make it
  a better place in which to live.
- Think about why you need these people.
- Think about how these people are paid
  for their work.

Firemen Visit School

One morning Miss Gay told
the Second Grade that the firemen
were coming to visit the school.

"Will they bring a fire truck?"
asked Sam.

"Yes, they will," said Miss Gay.

"We don't have a fire here," said Kate.
"Why are they coming?"

"They want to talk to us about fires,"
said Miss Gay. "They want to talk
about ways to prevent fires. They want
our help, too."

Everyone went out to see the firemen
and the fire truck. They looked
at everything.

They saw the fire hats and coats
the firemen wear.

They saw the red lights
and the big bell on the fire engine.

They saw the long fire hose.

Some of the children sat
in the front seat of the engine.
Some stood on the sides
where the firemen stand.

"Do you live at the fire station?"
Tom asked one of the firemen.

"We live at the fire station part
of the time," he said. "Some firemen
must be there all of the time.

We take turns living there.
We live there for a day and a night.
When we go home, other firemen
stay in our place."

"What do you do when there isn't
a fire?" asked Kate.

"We keep the fire engines
and fire fighting tools repaired," he said.

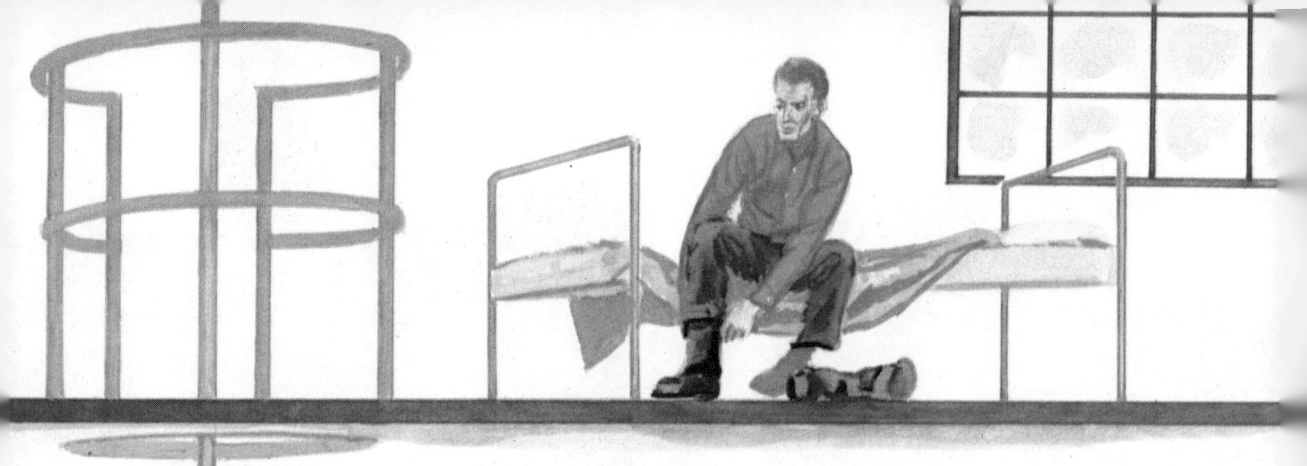

"Do you slide down a pole
when there is a fire?" asked Henry.

"Yes," said one of the firemen. "We
sleep upstairs at the fire station.

We put our clothes and boots near
our bed ready to put on. When there is
a fire, we must hurry. We dress
and slide down the pole very quickly."

"How do you know where the fire is?"
asked Sue.

"Sometimes people telephone and tell
us where the fire is," said the fireman.

"Sometimes the fire alarm bell rings
and the fire alarm machine
shows a number. This number tells us
where the fire is."

117

"Do all of the firemen ride to the fire
on this truck?" asked Sam.

"Not always," answered one
of the firemen. "If the fire is small,
we send this truck. If the fire is big,
we send the hook and ladder truck, too."

"This truck is a pumper truck,"
said another fireman. "We carry water
in this truck for small fires.
For big fires, we get water
from a fire hydrant.

The hook and ladder truck has long
ladders. We can use the ladders
to fight fires in big buildings."

- Look at the picture on the next page.
- Can you name the different kinds
  of fire trucks?
- How do the firemen help to save people?
- How do the police help the firemen
  when there is a big fire?

Helping the Firemen

"There are cars that go to the fires,"
said a fireman.

"The fire chief has a red car,"
said Sam. "He always goes to the fires."

"That's right," said the fireman.
"There is another red car that goes
to the fires in Greenwood.
This car carries men
from fire insurance companies."

"Why do they go to fires?" asked Kate.

"They go to find out what started
the fires," said the fireman.

"Why do they want to know that?"
asked Sam.

"Fire insurance companies pay
for the buildings that catch on fire,"
said the fireman. "They want to be sure
that people are careful about fires."

"People who own big buildings and houses
buy fire insurance," said Miss Gay.

"They pay a little money each year
for fire insurance.

If a building burns down,
the insurance company will pay
for a new building. People
who do not have
fire insurance must pay
for their own new building.

Many, many people buy fire insurance,"
added Miss Gay. "Only a few people
have fires. This is why
the insurance company has enough money
to pay for new buildings and houses."

"We want to tell people in Greenwood
how to be careful about fires,"
said a fireman. "We need your help.

We want some pictures that show people
how to be careful about fires.

We are going to put these pictures
in stores and in schools.

We are asking many boys and girls
to help because we need many pictures.
Would you help us?"

"Yes, we will," said the children.

"I know you can think of many things
to tell the people," said the fireman.

Then the firemen said, "Good-by,"
to the boys and girls.

Miss Gay and the children talked
about the pictures they would make
for the firemen.

They thought of many pictures
that would tell people how to be careful
about fires.

Then everyone went to work
to make a picture.

Here are some of the pictures they made.

Do not play with matches.

Put out picnic fires
with sand or water.

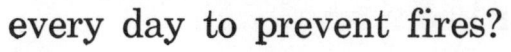
Keep the house clean.

Do not stand too near a fire.
Your clothes will burn.

- Can you think of other pictures
  you would draw?
- Can you think of things you could do
  every day to prevent fires?

Putting Out Fires Long Ago

Long ago men had different ways
of putting out fires.

People carried water by hand
from the well to the fire.

In some places today men
put out fires this way.

Do you know why?

The first fire trucks were small.

Then bigger fire trucks were built.
They used steam to pump the water.
They were faster than the hand pumps.

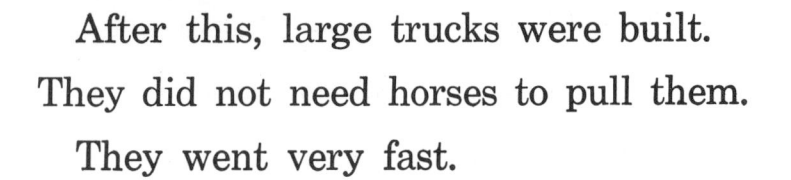

After this, large trucks were built.
They did not need horses to pull them.
They went very fast.

A New Fire Truck for Greenwood

New Fire Truck for Greenwood

Mayor Says No New Taxes Needed to Pay for Fire Truck.

A new hook and ladder truck will be bought for Greenwood. The Mayor and Council voted last night to buy a new fire truck. The truck will be ready next summer.

One morning Miss Gay brought something for the Second Grade. She found it in the Greenwood newspaper.

It told about a new fire truck for Greenwood. She showed it to the boys and girls.

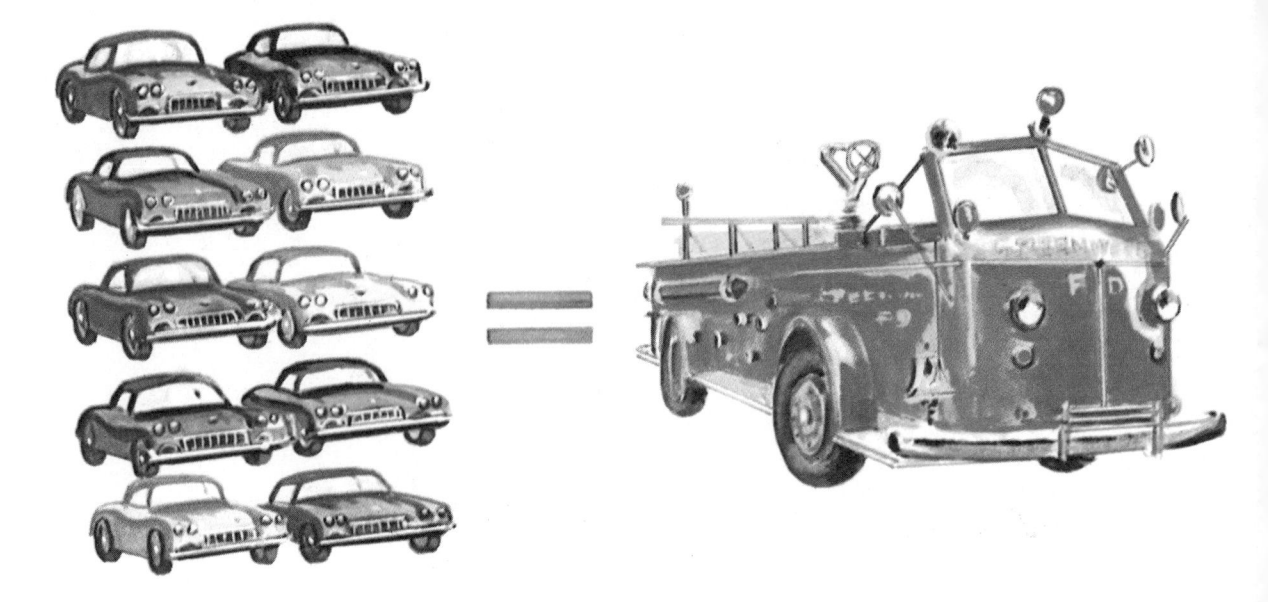

"Do you need a lot of money to buy a fire truck?" asked Tom.

"Yes," said Miss Gay. "It takes as much money as you would need to buy ten cars."

"That's a lot of money," said Tom.

"Do you know where Greenwood gets the money to pay for things we need?" asked Miss Gay.

"I think our mothers and fathers help pay for things in Greenwood," said Kate.

TAX MONEY PAYS FOR

Policemen

Firemen

Fire Engines

Schools and Teachers

"They do," said Miss Gay. "They pay taxes. All the people in Greenwood pay taxes on their homes and their stores.

They pay this money to Greenwood.

Greenwood will use the money to buy the fire truck.

The taxes are also used to pay the firemen and other people who work for Greenwood."

■ Can you think of other things that taxes pay for?

Police Help Make Greenwood Safe

"Policemen work for Greenwood,"
said Henry.

"Yes," said Miss Gay. "Policemen do
many things for the people of Greenwood."

"I know some of the things they do,"
said Kate.

"Policemen help us cross the street.
Policemen keep the cars from speeding."

- Can you tell what these policemen
  are doing?
- Can you think of any other things
  a policeman does?

"I want to be a policeman
when I grow up," said Henry.
"You will go to police school
to learn to be a policeman," said Miss Gay.
"Policemen must learn many things."

They must learn
all the laws in Greenwood.

They must learn to use
and take care of guns.

They must learn how
to help people who are hurt.

They must learn how
to direct traffic.

Teachers for Greenwood

"Miss Gay, do you work for Greenwood?"
asked Kate.

"Yes," said Miss Gay. "Teachers
in the public schools work for Greenwood.

Money from taxes is used to pay
public school teachers."

"Did you go to school to learn
to be a teacher?" asked Tom.

"Yes," said Miss Gay. "I went
to school for many years. There were
many things I had to learn in school."

■ Can you tell what Miss Gay is learning?

"Teachers work to help children learn," said Miss Gay. "There are other people who help us learn."

- Who are these people?
- How do they help us learn?
- Does money from taxes pay all of these people?

People Who Keep Greenwood Clean

"There are people who work to keep
Greenwood beautiful and clean,"
said Miss Gay.

"Garbage men help to keep
Greenwood clean," said Sue. "They take
the garbage from our house.

We put our garbage
in a big covered can. The garbage men put
the garbage in their truck.
Then they take it away."

"Yes," said Miss Gay. "They take
the garbage from all our houses."

- Who collects the garbage
  in your town or city?
- Can you find out where they take it?

"The men who work on the streets help us," said Tom. "They fixed a hole in our street yesterday."

"It takes many men to keep our streets fixed," said Miss Gay.

"They keep the streets clean too," said Sally. "Sometimes they wash the streets with a big water truck. I was splashed once."

"In winter they also help us," said Henry. "They plow the snow off the streets. I like to watch them push the snow to the side of the street."

- How are the streets
  in your city or town cleaned?
- Why should we keep the streets clean?
- How can you help to keep
  your streets clean?

"There are men who keep the parks clean and beautiful," said Miss Gay. "They cut the grass and plant flowers. These men work for Greenwood."

"I go to the park near my house," said Kate. "There are places to play. Sometimes I walk around and just look at the flowers."

"Sometimes I help the men pick up paper in the park," said Sam. "People throw it all over the ground. It makes the park look bad."

"That is one thing everyone can do to help keep our parks beautiful," said Miss Gay. "We can put paper in the baskets that are in the park."

- Do you have a park
  in your city or town?
- How can you make your park
  a better place for your neighbors?

Laws for Greenwood

"When people live together
in a city or town, they need rules
to help them live a better life,"
said Miss Gay.

"Rules like we have in a game?"
asked Henry.

"In a way," laughed Miss Gay.
"You need rules to tell you how
to play a game.

In Greenwood, we have rules
to help us live together. If everyone
follows these rules, then everyone
in Greenwood is happy.

We call these rules laws."

"I know a law," said Henry. "We
must not drive our cars too fast."

"Let's think of other laws we have
in Greenwood," said Miss Gay.

Do not park in front
of a fire hydrant.

Ride bicycles carefully
in the street.

Put your garbage
in covered cans.

- ■ Why do you think Greenwood needs
  these laws?
- ■ Can you think of other laws you have
  in your city or town?

"Who makes the laws for Greenwood?"
asked Sam.

"The mayor and councilmen make
the laws," said Miss Gay.

"They take care of the tax money
people pay to Greenwood. They buy
the things we need.

They pay the people who work
for Greenwood.

They do many things to help
all of us who live here.

The mayor and councilmen work
for Greenwood, too."

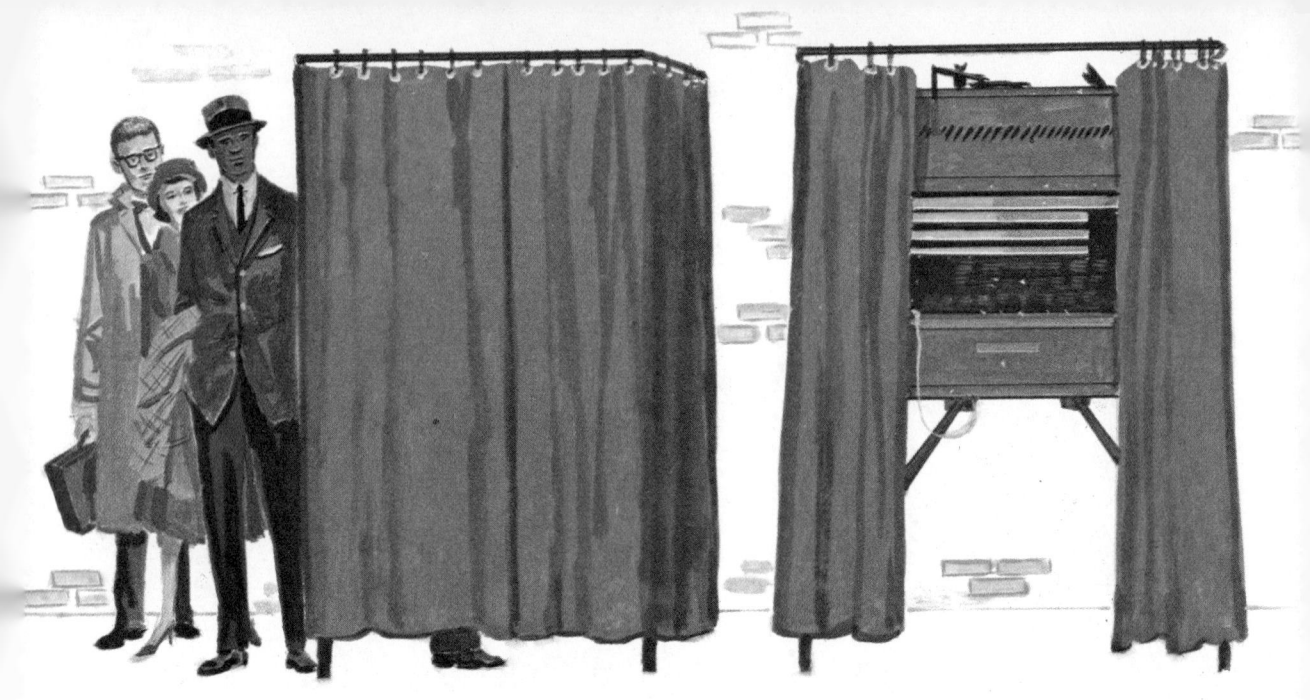

"Your mothers and fathers choose
these people.

All grown people in Greenwood vote.
They vote to choose the people they want
to make the laws.

People vote for the mayor and
councilmen."

- Do you have a mayor in your city
  or town?
- Who makes the laws for your city
  or town?

Who Works for Greenwood?

The Second Grade has learned about people
who work for Greenwood.

Money from taxes is used to pay
these people for their work.

Other people help their neighbors
in Greenwood. They are not paid
with tax money.

- Can you tell who works for
  your city or town and who does not?
- How are these people paid
  for their work?
- Can you think of other people
  who help you in your city or town?

Buildings

for Greenwood

Many people work to help us have
good homes and schools and stores.

In this part of the book,
the Second Grade will meet
some of these people in Greenwood.

They will learn about the people
who plan and put up buildings.

They will learn how electricity
and water get to the buildings
in Greenwood.

- As you read these stories,
  think about these things:
- Think about the people in your city
  or town who plan and put up buildings.
- Think about why these people
  are important to you.
- Think about how water and electricity
  get to your home.

New Schoolrooms

School Needs Space

Six New Rooms Needed

The Grade School has become too full. Plans have been made for six new rooms. People will vote to decide if they will be built.

"Look what I found in the newspaper," said Sam. "It's about our school."

"Daddy says we need more rooms," said Kate.

"Yes, we do," said Miss Gay. "Every room is full of children and some have too many."

"Will we have the new rooms soon?" asked Sam.

"The people who live here
must vote first," said Miss Gay.
"Maybe people will not vote Yes."

"But why not?" asked Sam.

"Taxes will go up a little,"
said Miss Gay. "Everyone will have
to pay more tax money."

"But we really need them," said Kate.

"Not everyone will think so,"
said Miss Gay.

"How can we tell people how much
we need the new rooms?" asked Sam.

"There will be more stories
about our rooms in the newspapers,"
said Miss Gay.

"They will tell how much we need
the new rooms.

They will tell how much more taxes
the people will have to pay.

Then each person will vote the way
he thinks is best."

Miss Gay told the Second Grade
to watch and see what the newspapers
said about the new rooms.

"You will find many other things
in the newspapers, too," she said.

"They have news about other towns
and countries.

They tell us about things
stores have to sell."

"Mother bought me a new dress
because we read about a sale," said Sue.

"We read about the weather and I like
to read the funny page," said Kate.

■ Can you think of other things
you will find in a newspaper?

"Many people work to make
a newspaper for us each day," said Miss Gay.

This man talks to people
to find out things to write.
He is called a reporter.

The reporter then
writes the story.

This man sets the type
for the newspaper. He
is called the typesetter.

This man helps
to print the newspaper.
He is called a pressman.

This boy sells
the newspapers to people.
He is called a newsboy.

"There are other ways people can hear about our new rooms," said Miss Gay.

"We can hear news over the radio and television," said Henry.

"Yes," said Miss Gay.

"As the day to vote comes closer, people will telephone to tell others to be sure to vote.

Some people will write letters to their neighbors about the new rooms. Some letters will say, Vote Yes. Other letters will say, Vote No.

We will not know if there will be new rooms until everyone votes."

- Bring something to school which you found in a newspaper.
- Tell the class some news you heard on the radio or television.

Planning the New Schoolrooms

"Miss Gay, the people voted Yes,"
said Kate. "We are going to have the
new schoolrooms."

"We can watch them work," said Sam.
"They are going to start right away."

A few days later, Tom came running
into school. "There's a bulldozer
outside," he said. "I saw it.

It is just like the one Ben and I
drove last summer. May we watch it?"

"Yes," said Miss Gay. "First let's
do our room jobs. Then we can go."

"Look at that bulldozer," said Tom.
"It can really push the dirt.

See those stakes, they tell the driver
how far to dig with his bulldozer."

"Who tells them where to put
the stakes?" asked Sally.

"I can answer that," said a man nearby.
"My friend and I heard you ask
about the stakes."

"Do you know about them?" asked Sally.

"Yes," said the man. "My plans
tell where the stakes go.
I am the architect
for the new schoolrooms."

"I drew a set of plans.
They are called blueprints.
Here is the blueprint
for the new schoolrooms."

"How does the blueprint tell
where the stakes go?" asked Sam.

"The blueprint tells how big
the rooms will be," said the architect.
"The workmen look at the blueprint
and mark the corners of the rooms
with the stakes.

The blueprint is like a map.
It shows the workmen where to build
the rooms. It shows where the doors
and windows will be."

An architect makes a blueprint
for everything that is built.

There are many different kinds
of architects.

- An architect's job is very important.
- Why must he be very careful
  in planning a building?
- Can you make a blueprint of something
  you would like to build?

Building the New Schoolrooms

"Here come two big trucks," said Sam.
"Is all that lumber for the new rooms?"

"Yes, it is," said the architect.
"Come with me. I will take you
to the contractor. He buys the lumber
and other things for the building."

"Hello," said the contractor.
"What can I do for you?"

"Do you know about those trucks?"
asked Sam.

"Yes, I do," said the contractor.
"Those trucks are from the lumberyard
in Greenwood. That is where I buy
my lumber."

"I visited a big forest last summer," said Sally. "We saw men cutting trees for lumber."

■ Can you tell the story of lumber?

"What else will you buy
for the new rooms?" asked Henry.

"We will need bricks,"
said the contractor. "I get bricks
at a brickyard. Bricks are made
from sand, clay, and water."

The sand, clay, and water
are mixed in big machines.

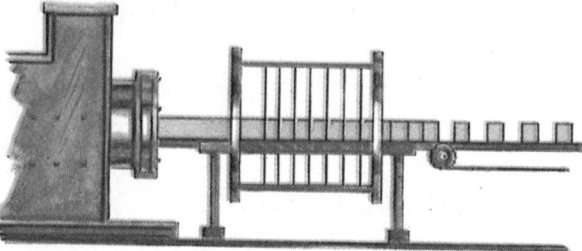

The bricks are baked
in an oven called a kiln.

There are different colors
and kinds of bricks."

"We buy concrete, too,"
said the contractor. "Soon a big truck
will bring concrete that is ready
for us to use."

"I have seen a truck like that,"
said Kate. "It has a big round top.
The top goes round and round."

"It mixes the concrete while it is
on the way to us," said the contractor.
"This will save us time in building
the new rooms."

The Second Grade watched the building
every day. One day they saw tall steel
beams go up in the air. The steel
will make the walls and roof strong.

Sam stopped to talk
to the contractor. He told Sam
that he bought the steel beams
from a steel mill.

The steel beams came by train
to Greenwood.

The Second Grade liked to watch the men
at work. They learned what each man did
to help build the new rooms.

■ Can you tell what these men did
to build the new rooms?

165

Electricity for the New Schoolrooms

"Where will the electricity
for the rooms come from?" asked Sam.

"It will come from the electric
power plant down near the river,"
said Miss Gay. "All the electricity
for Greenwood is made there.

We can visit the power plant.
You will see how the electric power
is made."

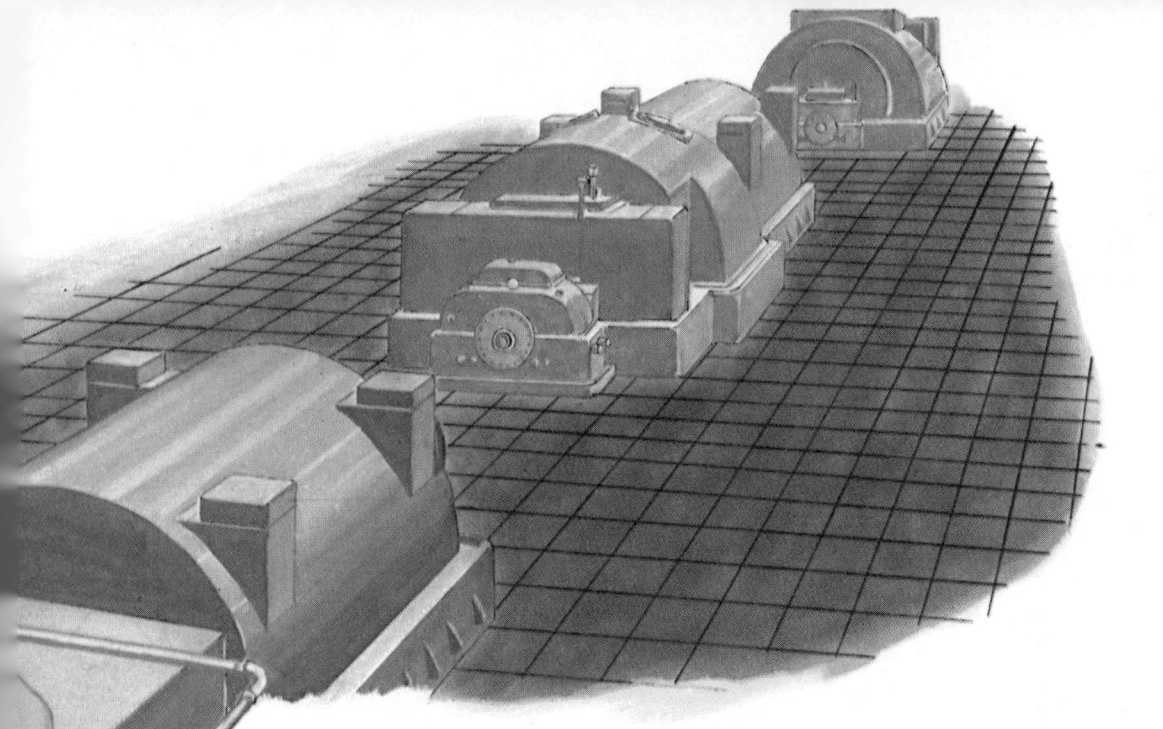

When they arrived at the power plant,
a man came to meet them.
His name was Mr. Henry.

"Hello," he said. "Would you like
to see our plant?"

"Yes, we want to see how you make
electricity here," said Sam.

"Come with me," said Mr. Henry.

"These machines make the electricity.
They are called generators. We need
three of these machines to make
enough electricity for Greenwood."

"Inside the generator are magnets,"
said Mr. Henry. "There are magnets
on the sides. There is
a big wheel in the middle.

The big wheel turns very fast.
As it turns, the magnets make electricity."

"What makes it go so fast?"
asked Sam.

"Steam makes it turn fast,"
answered Mr. Henry. "Steam is strong
and can push very hard and fast.
We have big fires that heat water
to make the steam for us."

"We make steam at our house
when we heat water," said Sue.

"We make steam the same way,"
said Mr. Henry. "Our fire is a big one
to make enough steam."

4. The wheel turns
between the magnets
to make electricity.

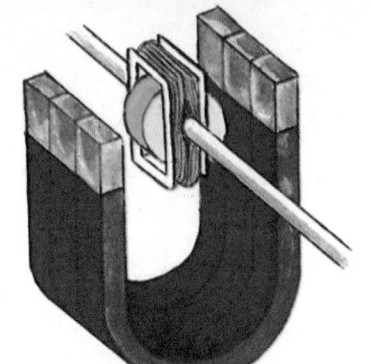

3. The steam makes
the wheel turn.

2. The water becomes steam.

1. Fire heats the water.

"Come with me," said Mr. Henry. "I will show you where the electricity goes from these machines."

Outside the power plant, Mr. Henry showed them the wires that carry the electricity.

"These big wires carry the electricity to Greenwood," he said.

"I would like to work up high like those men," said Sam.

"Those men have to be very careful," said Mr. Henry. "The electricity in the wires is very powerful. They wear heavy gloves and are careful when they work."

"Thank you, Mr. Henry," said Miss Gay. "We have learned something new today."

"Thank you," said the Second Grade as they got on the bus.

■ This is how electricity gets
from the power plant to Greenwood.

Power to Make Electricity

The Second Grade talked
about their visit to the power plant.
They wanted to see how steam can push
a wheel. Miss Gay helped them to see
how strong steam is.

They made a small wheel
like the big wheel that turns the generator.

They held the small wheel
over the steam.

- What do you think happened?
- Can you tell why?

"Power plants do not always use steam to make electricity," said Miss Gay.

"What do they use?" asked Kate.

"They use water from a river or lake," said Miss Gay.

"I saw a big dam out West," said Sally. "My father said dams hold back the water until it is needed to make electricity."

"Yes," said Miss Gay. "When the water is needed, it falls from a high dam.

When water falls from a high dam, it is very strong.

It makes the wheels go very fast."

DAM

WATER

GENERATOR

■ This is how water is used to make electricity.

When Sue came to school the next day she said, "My father showed me the electric meter at our house."

"Do you know why you have an electric meter?" asked Miss Gay.

"Yes," said Sue. "It tells how much electricity we use. We have to pay for the electricity we use."

"I watched the man from the electric company," said Sam.
"He comes and reads our meter. Then the company sends my father a card telling how much he must pay."

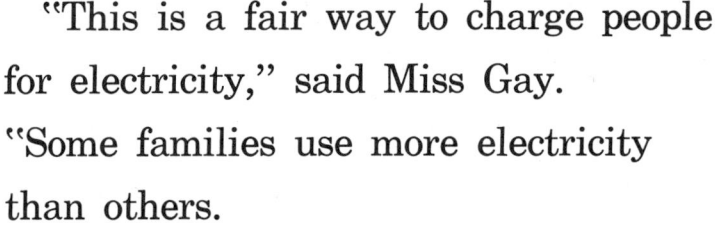

"This is a fair way to charge people for electricity," said Miss Gay. "Some families use more electricity than others.

Everyone pays for the electricity he uses.

We all have many things that are run by electricity," said Miss Gay.

"Electricity is something we all use every day."

- Count all the things in your home that are run by electricity.

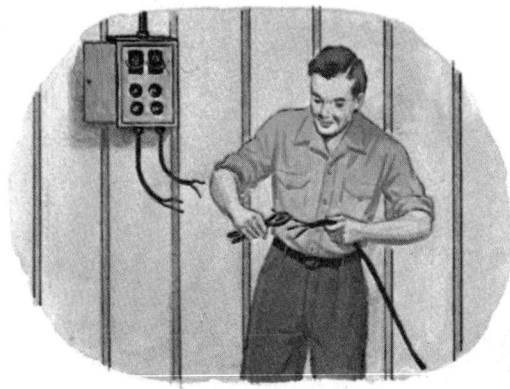

- Many people help us get electricity.
- Can you tell what these people do to help you?

Water for the New Schoolrooms

Sam and Kate saw Miss Gay walking
to school.

"Hi," they called as they crossed
the street.

"Good morning," said Miss Gay. "This
is such a beautiful morning.
I am enjoying my walk."

"We are too," said Kate.

"Look at the new machine in front
of the school," called Sam. "I wonder
what it is doing there."

"Let's walk faster and we can find
out," said Kate.

Tom, Henry, and Sue were already watching the big machine.

"What are they doing with the machine?" asked Sam.

"They are digging so they can put down water pipes," answered Tom.

"These pipes are for the new schoolrooms," said Sue.

"Where will the water come from?" asked Sam.

"I know," said Tom. "The man said there was a big pipe under the street. This pipe will take the water from the big pipe to the schoolrooms."

179

"My father works where they pump the water for Greenwood," said Henry.

"What does your father do there?" asked Miss Gay.

"He helps to make the water clean," said Henry.

"How does he clean the water?" asked Sam.

"I don't know," said Henry.

"Do you think your father would come to school and tell us about our water in Greenwood?" asked Miss Gay.

"Oh, yes," said Henry. "I know he would like to."

Mr. Hill Visits the Second Grade

Henry's father came to visit
the Second Grade.

"This is Mr. Hill," said Miss Gay.
"You may ask him some of the things
you wanted to know about water."

"Where does our water come from?"
asked Bob.

"How do you clean it?" asked Sue.

"The water for Greenwood comes
from under the ground," said Mr. Hill.
"We dig deep holes in the ground
to reach water. They are called wells."

"Then we put big pumps over the wells,"
said Mr. Hill. "These pumps are very large
and are run by electricity.

When the pump pulls the water up,
we send it in big pipes to a building
that is nearby.

In this building we make the water
clean and pure. The water goes through
sand to make it clean. Then we add
something to help make the water pure.

Then the water is pumped
into a high water tank. It stays there
until people use it."

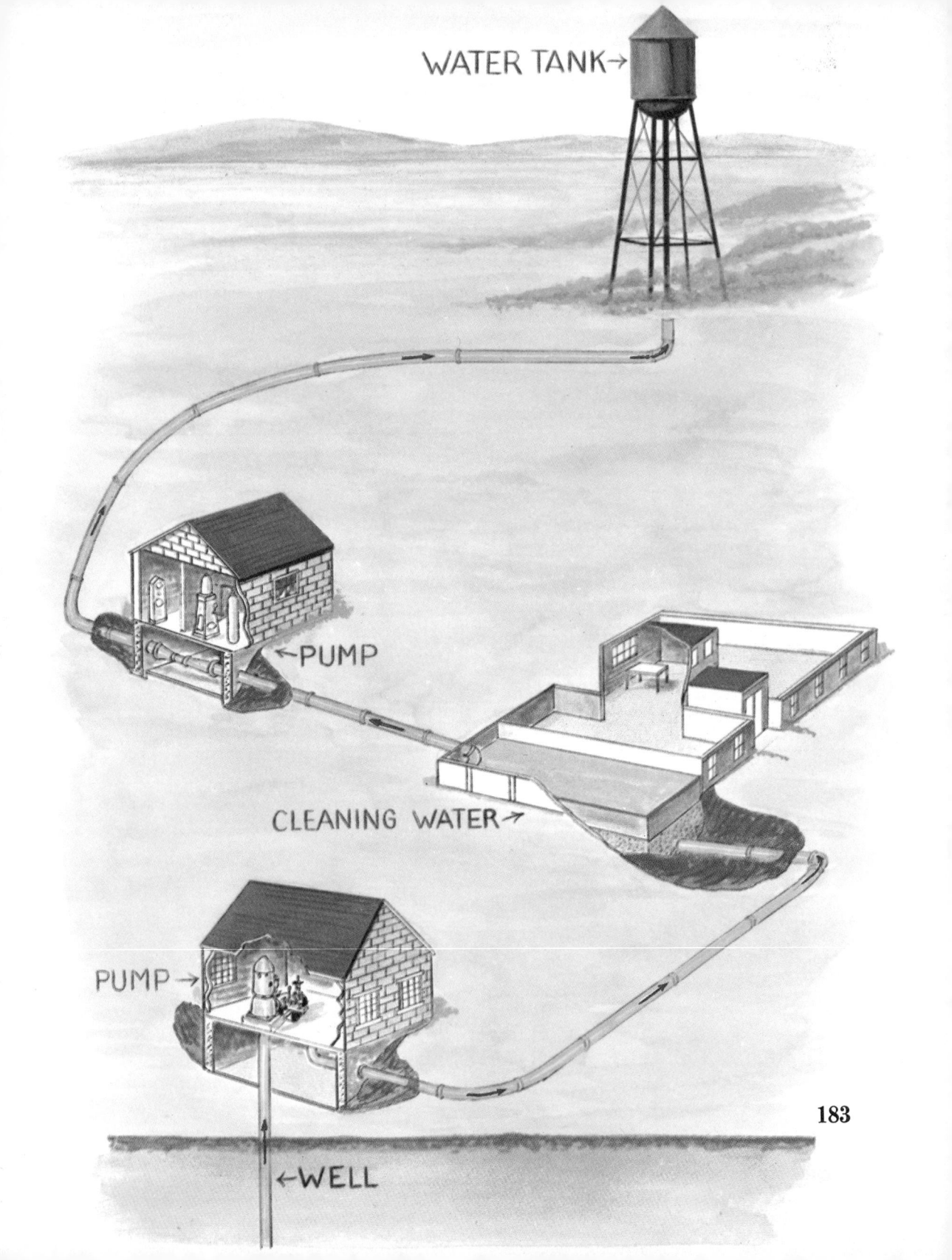

WATER TANK→

←PUMP

CLEANING WATER↗

PUMP→

183

←WELL

"The water goes from the tank to the homes and buildings of Greenwood. Because this tank is high, the water goes very fast."

"Thank you for coming," said Miss Gay. "You have helped us very much."

"I was very glad to come," said Mr. Hill.

"Thank you and good-by,"
said the Second Grade.

- Why do you think sand is used to help clean the water for Greenwood?
- Why is water put into a high tank when it is ready for people to use?

Other People Who Help Water Get to You

There are men who lay
pipes in the ground
to new houses.

There are men who help
to bring the water inside
the new houses.

This man comes to your house
to see how much water
you have used. Who pays
for your water?

- How does your city or town
  get water?
- How else do people get water?

Water Long Ago

People long ago had different ways
of getting water.

- Can you tell how these different people
  got water?

Who Are Our Neighbors?

The Second Grade has learned many things about their neighbors in Greenwood.

They have learned that their neighbors are the people who live near them.

They know that neighbors do things for each other. They help each other get the things they need every day.

They know that people who do not live near them also help them.

■ Which of these people are neighbors to the Second Grade?

■ Can you remember what these people do
to help their neighbors in Greenwood?

You have been learning
about your own city or town.

Tell about the different places
to buy food in your city or town.

Where do the people in your city
or town get their clothes?

Are there any factories?
What do they make?

Are there any farms? What is raised
on them?

How do things from far away get
to your city or town?

What people protect
you and your neighbors?

What people help you
and your neighbors learn?

What people make your city or town
clean and beautiful?

What can you do to help these people?

Who makes the laws in your city or town?

Which laws do you think are best?

What new buildings are
in your city or town? Did you watch
them being built? How were they built?
Where did the builders get the lumber
and other things for the buildings?

Where does your city or town
get electricity? Do you know
how it is made?

Where does your water come from?
Where is the water tank
for your city or town?

Tell all the ways you and your neighbors
get the news. How many newspapers
are there in your city or town? Do you
know the people who deliver the newspapers
in your neighborhood?

Do you know how your city or town
looked many years ago? Can you find
pictures that show you?

Do you think your city or town
will look different next year? Why?

WORD
LIST

Careful attention has been given to the readability of this text. Sentences are not complicated and are arranged so that ideas are easily followed.

Word selection has been geared to the reading level of the second grade reader. Special terms and phrases for conveying the social studies ideas have been used. These are listed below by the pages on which they first occur. Teachers may wish to introduce these words to the children before they meet them in the text.

Page	Word or Term
6	waiting
7	ranch
8	map
9	airplane
	traveled
10	decided
11	ropes
	pointed
12	hours
	airport
	apart
13	— —
14	— —
15	roundup
	cattle
	brand
	mark
	Bar Z
16	calves
17	— —
18	Supplies
19	different
20	New York City
	thirteen
21	station
	taxi
	policeman
22	subway
	hundreds
23	ridden
24	model
	Statue of Liberty
25	neighborhood
26	bulldozer
	lemonade
27	— —
28	roared
29	— —

Page	Word or Term
30	house trailer
	bedrooms
	bathroom
	kitchen
31	trailer park
	Grand Canyon
	desert
32	mountain
	fire tower
	forest ranger
33	careful
	prevent
34	vacation
35	library
	rocket
36	airplane hangars
	control tower
	pilot
37	— —
38	— —
39	— —
40	Greenwood
41	apartment houses
	together
42	— —
43	— —
44	— —
45	— —
46	— —
47	supermarket
	storerooms
48	principal
49	downstairs
50	unload
	slide
	groceries
51	upstairs
	main floor

Page	Word or Term
	machine
52	refrigerators
53	frozen
54	ax
55	fruits
	vegetables
	fresh
56	butchers
	tools
57	Produce
58	California
	Florida
59	— —
60	leaves
	lettuce
	wrapped
61	chocolate
	piece
62	cacao tree
	countries
	pods
	cacao beans
	equator
63	— —
64	knife
65	ocean
66	factory
	ovens
	melts
	liquid
	cocoa butter
67	sugar
68	— —
69	juice
70	— —
71	— —
72	bakery
73	bakers